the
Goddess
within

Compiled by River Huston

Illustrated by Patricia Languedoc

Running Press
PHILADELPHIA · LONDON

A Running Press Miniature Edition™

Printed in China

Library of Congress Cataloging-in-Publication Number 98-68476

ISBN 0-7624-0530-9

This book may be ordered by mail from the publisher. Please include $1.00 for postage and handling. ***But try your bookstore first!***

Running Press Book Publishers
125 South Twenty-second Street
Philadelphia, Pennsylvania 19103-4399

Visit us on the web!
www.runningpress.com

Contents

Introduction

The ancient goddess is every-
where—within all of us and in
all that surrounds us. Her wisdom
comes to us through imagery
in painting, sculpture, dance,
literature, music, poetry, science,
athletics, film, architecture,
and all creative endeavors. To see
her influence, you need only look.
She has always been here.

At times, the goddess has been banished or burned; yet still she has endured. With every reemergence, she guides us to a place where we can see beyond the man-made lines on our planet, the color of our skin,  the shape of our bodies, and what we call ourselves. She imparts a wisdom that challenges society's stereotypical

images and reveals the true essence
of woman—profound strength,
deep compassion, consummate love,
and unfailing justice.

Within these pages, modern
goddesses offer insight, attitude,
passion, and inspiration through
their words and actions. Turn
to their powerful voices to find
guidance, spirituality, strength,
and solace . . . and then pass it on.

the
Attitude

The one thing that does
not abide by majority's
rule is a person's conscience.

Harper Lee

I think the reward
for conformity
is everyone likes you
but yourself.

Rita Mac Brown

Until you've lost your reputation, you never realize what a burden it was, or what freedom really is.

Margaret Mitchell

I survived
because I was
tougher than
everyone else.

Bette Davis

Goddess ....

I am tough, ambitious,
and I know what I want.
If that makes me a bitch, okay.
I can throw a fit,
I am a master at it.

Madonna

It is time to stop
denying the inner
bitch in ourselves.
Stop apologizing
for her. Set her free.

Elizabeth Hilts

Success didn't spoil
me, I've always
been insufferable.

Fran Lebowitz

What I wanted to be when
I grew up was in charge.

Wilma Vaught

The militant
not the meek shall
inherit the earth.

Mother Jones

The pain of leaving
those you love is only
a prelude to under-
standing yourself.

Shirley MacLaine

I want the freedom to carve
and chisel my own face,
to staunch the bleeding with
ashes, to fashion my own
Gods from my entrails.

Gloria Anzualdua

In my long and colorful career,
one thing stands out:
I have been misunderstood.

Mae West

In my life's chain
of events, nothing
was accidental.

Hannah Senesh

*All the women
I know feel a
little like outlaws.*

Marilyn French

Goddess ....

I have bursts of being a lady,
but it doesn't last long.

Shelley Winters

I never practice,
I only play.

Wanda Landowska

*If you don't
want to get old,
don't mellow.*

Linda Ellerbee

"Afraid" is a country
with no exit visa.

Audre Lorde

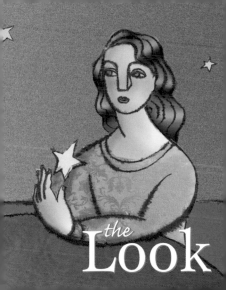

the
Look

I deliberately overeat to give my body the most voluptuous contours I can acquire. Growing fatter is one of the most intensely sensuous things that I have ever experienced.

Margaret Deidre O'Hartigan

No one can make
you feel inferior
without your consent.

Eleanor Roosevelt

Beauty comes in all
shapes and sizes.
Our goals should be
health [and] stamina.

Emme Aronson

My nipples are
in their prime.

Sandra Bernhard

Why do I show my cervix?
Because it's fun—and
I think fun is really important.

Annie Sprinkle

Women should try to increase
their size rather than
decrease it, because the bigger
we are the more space
we take up and the more we
have to be reckoned with.

Roseanne Barr

Elegance does not
consist of putting
on a new dress.

Coco Chanel

*I base most of my
fashion taste
on what doesn't itch.*

Gilda Radnor

I always wear slacks
because of the
brambles and maybe
the snakes.

Katharine Hepburn

*If I can't have too many truffles,
I will do without.*

Colette

I do not lose myself all at once.
I rubbed out my face
over the years. Washing away
my pain. The same
way carvings on stone are
worn down by water.

Amy Tan

Don't deprive
me of my age.
I have earned it.

May Sarton

*It's more important
what's in a woman's
face than what's on it.*

Claudette Colbert

*One cannot
have wisdom
without living life.*

Dorothy McCall

Surviving meant
being born
over and over.

Erica Jong

There are as many
ways to live and grow
as there are people.

Evelyn Mandel

I like trees because
they seem more resigned
to the way they have
to live than other things do.

Willa Cather

There is a period of life where
we swallow a knowledge
of ourselves and it becomes
either good or sour inside.

Pearl Bailey

Don't compromise yourself; you are all you got.

Janis Joplin

No trumpets sound
when the important
decisions in our life
are made. Destiny is
made known silently.

Agnes DeMille

I didn't notice
I was a woman.
I regard myself as
the prime minister.

Margaret Thatcher

People call me a feminist
whenever I express sentiments
that differentiate me from
a doormat or a prostitute.

Rebecca West

When I am alone I am not
aware of my race or my sex,
both in need of social
context for definition.

Maxine Hong Kingston

No matter how
cynical you get it is
impossible to keep up.

Lily Tomlin

We make ourselves up as we go.

Kate Green

Old age is like flying
through a storm.
Once you're aboard
there is nothing
you can do.

Golda Meir

*Toleration is
the greatest gift
of the mind.*

Helen Keller

There is nothing
stronger
than gentleness.

Han Suyin

You can no more
win a war
than you can win
an earthquake.

Jeannette Rankin

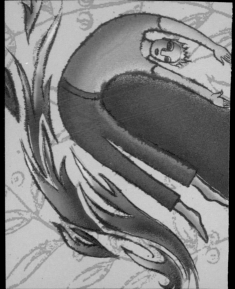

Loving

The brother that gets me is going to get one hell of a woman.

Aretha Franklin

A girl can wait for the right
man to come along; but
in the meantime that still
doesn't mean she can't
have a wonderful time
with all the wrong ones.

Cher

Don't start dating
someone just because
you are too lazy
to commit suicide.

Judy Tenuta

It is ridiculous to think that you can spend your entire life with just one person. Three is about the right number. Yes, I imagine three husbands would do it.

Clare Boothe

Goddess ....

*In love there are
two things,
bodies and words.*

Joyce Carol Oates

All great lovers are articulate,
and verbal seduction is the
surest road to actual seduction.

Marya Mannes

The requirements
of romantic love are
difficult to satisfy
in the back seat
of a Dodge Dart.

Lisa Alther

When one is pretending, the entire body revolts.

Anaïs Nin

A mutual and satisfied sexual
act is of great benefit to the
average woman; the magnetism
of it is health-giving.

Margaret Sanger

On sex:
Unless there is an
emotional tie,
I'd rather play tennis.

Bianca Jagger

In America,
sex is an obsession;
in other
parts of the world,
it is a fact.

Marlene Dietrich

Something is wrong here:
sex has been with us since
the human race began,
yet I would estimate that ninety
percent of human beings
still suffer from enormous
inhibitions in this area.

Xaviera Hollander

No one has ever
loved anyone
the way everyone
wants to be loved.

Mignon McLaughlin

Love is the extremely difficult
realization that something
other than one's self is real.

Dame Iris Murdoch

Never go to bed mad.
Stay up and fight.

Phyllis Diller

Sometimes it is
worse to win
a fight than lose.

Billie Holiday

Loving, like prayer,
is a power as well as a process.
It is curative. It is creative.

Zona Gale

Love is not enough.
It must be
the foundation,
the cornerstone,
but not the
complete structure.

Bette Davis

We tend to think of the erotic as
an easy, tantalizing sexual
arousal. I speak of the erotic as
the deepest life force, a force
which moves up towards living
in a fundamental way.

Audre Lorde

If it is your time,
love will track you
down like a cruise
missile. If you say
"I don't want it right
now," that's when you
will get it for sure.

Linda Barry

*It is better to die
on your feet than live
on your knees.*

Delores Ibarruri

The biggest sin is
sitting on your ass.

Florynce Kennedy

I don't waste time thinking,
"Am I doing it right?"
I ask, "Am I doing it?"

Georgette Mosbacher

You must do the thing
that you think
you cannot do.

Eleanor Roosevelt

If you are not
living on the edge,
you are taking
up too much room.

Lorraine Teel

The need for
change bulldozed
a road down the
center of my mind.

Maya Angelou

A life of reaction is a life
of slavery, intellectually and
spiritually. One must fight
for a life of action, not reaction.

Rita Mae Brown

Once I decide to do something,
I can't have people telling me
I can't. If there is a roadblock,
you jump over it, walk
around it, crawl under it.

Kitty Kelly

When people tell you that
you can't do something,
you kind of want to try it.

Margaret Chase Smith

Well-behaved women
rarely make history.

Laurel Thatcher Ulrich

I have no regrets. I wouldn't
have lived my life the way I did
if I were going to worry about
what people were going to say.

Ingrid Bergman

Everyone has talent.
What is rare is
the courage to follow
the talent to the
dark place it leads.

Erica Jong

A small group of
thoughtful people can
change the world.
Indeed it is the only
thing that ever has.

Margaret Mead

You don't get to choose how you are going to die. Or when. You can only decide how you're going to live. Now.

Joan Baez

As she stood before
the firing squad:
Life is an illusion.

Mata Hari

This book has been bound
using handcraft methods and
Smyth-sewn to ensure durability.

The dust jacket and interior were
designed by Corinda Cook.

The text was edited by Greg Jones.

The cover and interior illustrations
were done by Patricia Languedoc.

The text was set in
Esprit and Caflisch.